Introdu

The Berwyn Range & the Ceirio
relatively unknown area of Nort
opportunities, free from the crowds. Th
upland landscape of mountain, hills a
of it now Open Access land. Part of it i
an important habitat for Black Grouse and birds of prey. The highest peak
is Cadair Berwyn (2722 feet) and nearby is Pistyll Rhaeadr, at 240 feet, the
highest waterfall in England and Wales.

From its heart flows the Ceiriog river, which meanders eastwards from
Llanarmon Dyffryn Ceiriog beneath part wooded slopes and rolling hills
through Glyn Ceiriog to the border town of Chirk. The area has a network of
ancient highways used by monks from Valle Crucis Abbey and later drovers.
The valley once bustled with activity from fulling mills, mines, large dolerite
and slate quarries. It even had its own narrow gauge railway, the Glyn Valley
Tramway (1873-1935), linking the Glyn Ceiriog area to Chirk. In 1923 plans
to build two reservoirs in the upper valley to supply water to Warrington
were stopped, with the intervention of the Prime Minister, Lloyd George, who
described the Ceiriog Valley as 'a little bit of heaven on earth'! Today it retains
its beauty, tranquility and Welsh cultural heritage. Yet despite its closeness to
the busy A5 and the border, it remains little visited, unlike the Dee Valley just
to the north.

The 32 walks in this book range from an easy 1¾ mile stroll around Chirk
Castle estate to a challenging 13 mile Berwyn Mountain ridge walk. They
follow public rights of way and permissive paths, or cross Open Access land.
They incorporate sections of several waymarked local routes: the Ceiriog
Valley Walk, the multi-user Ceiriog Trail and Upper Ceiriog Trail, the new
North Berwyn Way from Corwen to Llangollen, and the Offa's Dyke Path.
Many individual routes, as well as containing shorter walk options, can easily
be linked with others, to provide longer day walks, if required.

Be properly prepared and equipped, especially for the higher mountain/
moorland routes, where weather conditions can quickly change. Walking
boots are required, along with appropriate clothing to protect against the
elements. Please remember that path conditions can vary according to season
and weather.

Each walk has a detailed map and description, but bear in mind though
that changes in detail can occur at any time. The location of each walk is
shown on the back cover and a summary of their key features is also given.
This includes an estimated walking time, but allow more time to enjoy the
scenery and sights.

Please observe the country code. Enjoy your walking!

CHIRK

DESCRIPTION A 5 mile walk (**A**) around Chirk, featuring a crossing of Telford's stunning aqueduct, famous early 18thC ornamental wrought-iron gates, and a visit to Chirk Castle via a white waymarked permissive footpath (open 1st April – 30th September) and red waymarked Estate trail. Allow about 3 hours. Check castle opening days/times (01691 777701). Dogs must be on leads and are not allowed in the castle or garden. A shorter 2¼ mile walk (**B**) omitting the castle is included.
START Chirk car park SJ 291377.
DIRECTIONS The car park is signposted from the B5070 along Colliery Road.

C hirk stands in Wales overlooking the border with England. Its strategic importance is evidenced by a 12thC Norman castle and the more famous Chirk castle to the west. Chirk is also situated on Thomas Telford's historic London to Holyhead turnpike road, along which stagecoaches carried the Irish Mail. Coal mining has been important to the town and surrounding area since the 16thC, with the last local colliery closing in 1968.

I From the far end of the car park, walk through the 'no exit' and car park of the Hand Hotel, an early 19thC coaching inn, to reach the High Street. Follow the road south through Chirk past St Mary's parish church, parts of which date from the 12thC. *Behind The Mount, the prominent 18thC three storey house on the corner, is the site of the Norman motte and bailey castle which protected the ford over the river Ceiriog. In 1164 it resisted Henry II, whose army was subsequently defeated by the Welsh at Crogen 2 miles to the west of Chirk.* Continue down the pavement on the B5070 to cross a stile on the left. Follow the path down the hillside to cross a stile by an old leat and on to rejoin the B5070 at the entrance to Seventh Heaven, a former mill.

2 Turn LEFT along the pavement, soon crossing the river Ceiriog. Cross the road

with care to the Bridge Inn and continue up the side road to reach the Llangollen canal. Turn RIGHT and walk alongside the canal, past cottages and across the aqueduct. *This splendid 10 arched structure carrying the canal 70 feet above the Ceiriog valley was designed by Thomas Telford, the great engineer, and completed in 1801. Nearby is the railway viaduct built by Henry Robertson in 1846-48 for the Chester-Shrewsbury railway line. It was made deliberately higher than the aqueduct to emphasise the superiority of rail over water! Due to the objection of Colonel Robert Myddleton Biddulph of Chirk Castle it was built at night! Both are built of local yellow sandstone.* At the other side you enter Wales. Ahead is the entrance to the mile long Chirk tunnel. Take the path angling up to the road. Turn LEFT and go along the B4500 towards Glyn Ceiriog. Shortly take a path angling off the road on the right through trees, then follow the perimeter of a caravan park round to its entrance. Continue along the road to a junction by impressive early 18th C ornamental gates and screen. *Known locally as 'The Pretty Gates', they were made by the Davies brothers of Bersham and originally stood at the north front of the castle.* Go along the road ahead signposted to Chirk Castle.

3 Shortly you have a choice. (For **Walk B** take the signposted path through a kissing gate on the right. Go down the field to another kissing gate, then bear RIGHT through the wood to the road. Follow it LEFT past the station and along Station Avenue into Chirk.) For **Walk A**, just beyond, turn LEFT along a track on the signed permissive footpath to Chirk Castle. After a kissing gate keep ahead past a wood, then alongside the fence to another kissing gate. Now go half-RIGHT up across the parkland to a kissing gate in the fence corner. Turn LEFT, go through another kissing gate and follow the waymarked path alongside railings, up past the wood and across the field – *with your first view of Chirk Castle* – to a stile. Continue ahead along the driveway. When it splits take the left fork. (If wishing to visit the castle first buy tickets at nearby Home Farm.) Shortly, take the lane up towards the castle, then just before seats at a red-topped post, take a path on the right. Follow the red waymarked path through woodland, then across parkland to eventually join your out-

ward route back to the road. (See **Walk 2** for detailed description.) Turn RIGHT, then go through the nearby kissing gate to join **Walk B** back to Chirk.

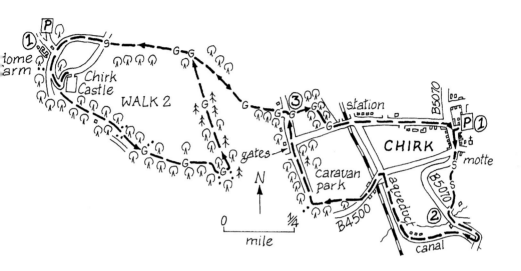

WALK 2

CHIRK CASTLE

DESCRIPTION A 1¾ mile walk around Chirk Castle, its estate and woodland, on a red way-marked Estate trail, complementing a visit to this splendid 14thC castle and its formal gardens. Open March – October, but check days/times (01691 777701). Dogs must be on leads and are not allowed in the castle or garden.
START Car park, Chirk Castle SJ 267383.
DIRECTIONS The castle lies to the west of Chirk and is well signposted.

*T*he castle *was completed in 1310 by Roger Mortimer for Edward 1 after the conquest of Wales. Similar in design to Beaumaris, it was one of a chain of border castles built to reinforce English dominance. Now managed by the National Trust, it has been continuously occupied by the Myddleton family since 1595. Running*

through the castle grounds is Offa's Dyke, built about 790 AD.

For visiting the castle or garden, please first obtain your tickets from nearby Home Farm Visitor Centre, then go through the arch-way to the road. Follow it RIGHT, soon taking a lane up towards the castle. After visiting the castle, return down to a red-topped post just below seats, then take the path angling back through trees. Shortly, take the right fork down to a track just above the road. Follow it LEFT to go through a red marked gate. The path continues along the wood/field edge, later bending RIGHT to go through a red marked gate on the left. It now passes through mature mixed woodland to another gate, then crosses park-land to a kissing gate in the far fence corner by a small wood. The waymarked path continues west to another kissing gate, then alongside railings, up past a wood and across the field to a stile onto the driveway. Follow the driveway ahead back to the start.

WALK 3

OFFA'S DYKE & CHIRK CASTLE

DESCRIPTION A 6½ mile walk exploring the attractive undulating countryside near Chirk. The route initially follows the Ceiriog Valley Walk to reach a section of the original 8thC Offa's Dyke. After a 1½ miles on the Offa's Dyke Path, it returns via a waymarked permissive path (open 1st April – 30th September) across Chirk Castle estate with the option of visiting the Castle (check opening times). Allow about 3½ hours.
START Chirk car park SJ 291377.
DIRECTIONS See Walk 1.

1 Follow instructions in paragraph **1** of **Walk 1**.

2 Go through a kissing gate opposite, then continue across the field near the Ceiriog river to pass under the massive stone aqueduct and railway viaduct (See **Walk 1** for information). Continue along the river bank to eventually reach a road junction. Turn LEFT across Pont Faen – *the oldest stone bridge in the Ceiriog valley and once an important crossing on the Chester to Cardiff road* – then turn RIGHT along the narrow road to cross a stile on the right opposite the first cottage. Follow the path through the meadow, soon joining the river. Continue through two further fields to enter a Woodland Trust wood. Follow the path through the trees above the river and up a long stepped section, later leaving the wood by a stile. After another stile, the path continues to gates by outbuildings of a cottage. Go up its access track to a minor road. Turn RIGHT, then take the waymarked path on the left past The Old School House (*built in 1871, closed in the 1960s*) to a stile. Just beyond, the waymarked path turns LEFT through a gap in the hedge, crosses undulating ground, goes through a tree boundary, and on to a stile. Follow an enclosed track LEFT up to the bend of a lane.

3 Turn sharp RIGHT along another track – *with a view of Chirk Castle* – soon rising and continuing across the part wooded hillside to join Offa's Dyke Path by an information board beneath an impressive section of original embanked dyke. Cross the stile on the right and descend the long field, initially near the dyke and past two houses to cross stiles in the field bottom. Descend a hedged track, then follow the path down to the road. Go down the road opposite, over the river, to reach the B4500. Follow Offa's Dyke Path up the no through road opposite and across the part wooded hillside, later passing a large house and rising steadily to end at a farm. The National Trail continues up the stony path, soon crossing a stile up on the right, then goes up the field to a stile. Follow the stiled field path – *enjoying another view of Chirk Castle* – to a road. Turn RIGHT.

4 On the bend take the National Trust permissive path past the nearby house, and through several fields, then along a track past the car park to Home Farm Visitor Centre, where tickets for the castle are available. If you are not visiting the castle, take the no exit road bending left. At a junction cross a stile ahead. Follow the white/red topped path across the field, past a wood. After a second kissing gate angle away from the corner down the parkland to a kissing gate. Go down alongside the fence and on past a wood to a kissing gate to reach the nearby road. Turn RIGHT, then go through a kissing gate on the left. Go down the field to another kissing gate, then bear RIGHT through the wood to the road. Follow it LEFT past the station and along Station Avenue into Chirk.

WALK 4

OFFA'S DYKE & CANAL

DESCRIPTION A 9 mile walk of great variety, which extends the outward route of Walk 3 via Offa's Dyke Path to the Llangollen Canal, which it follows back to Chirk via a short tunnel (railed but a torch is useful). Allow about 4½ hours.
START Chirk car park SJ 291377.

1 – 3
Follow instructions in **Walk 3**.

4 Continue along the road. Later Offa's Dyke Path crosses two fields, then continues along another road, soon taking its right fork. At crossroads keep ahead, then after ¼ mile follow Offa's Dyke Path through two fields to the A5. Cross the road with care, turn RIGHT, then LEFT along a track, past

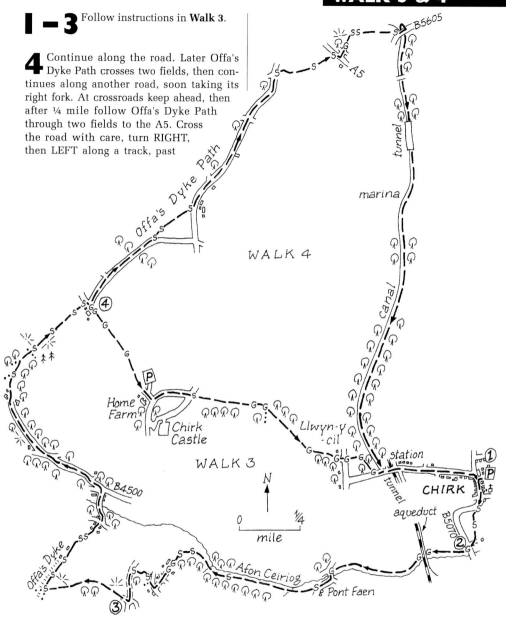

the entrance to Cloud Hill, to a gate. Go along the field edge, over a stile in the bottom corner, and another nearby. Go along the long field with the Llangollen canal below to reach the B5605. Turn LEFT then follow Offa's Dyke Path down to the canal. Now follow the towpath back under the road and south towards Chirk, passing through Whitehouse Tunnel (174 metres), passing Chirk marina, then along a wooded section of canal. Just before Chirk tunnel take the path up to the road. Turn LEFT, past the station and continue ahead along Station Avenue into Chirk.

WALK 5

COED PEN-CRAIG & OFFA'S DYKE

DESCRIPTION A 5¼ mile walk (**A**) exploring hills south-east of Pontfadog, featuring an impressive short section of the 8thC Offa's Dyke and good views of Chirk Castle. The route follows a track up through woodland above Cwm Gwryd into open country, reaching a height of 1174 feet, before joining the Offa's Dyke Path. It then follows an old track and field paths to join a section of the Ceiriog Valley Walk back to Pontfadog. Allow about 3 hours. The route can easily be shortened to a 4¼ mile walk (**B**).

START Car park, Pontfadog SJ 234380.

DIRECTIONS Ponfadog lies on on the B5400 about 4 miles from Chirk. The riverside car park is on the left just beyond the Post Office/stores.

O ffa's Dyke originally extended from the sea at Prestatyn southwards to the Severn estuary, near Chepstow. It marked the boundary between the Saxon kings of Mercia and the independent kingdoms of Wales. It was named after the Mercian king Offa (757-796) in whose reign it was built. The dyke consisted of an earthen bank up to 8 metres high with a ditch to the west, and was a considerable feat of engineering. About 80 miles of the ancient earthwork can still be recognised today.

I From the top of the car park cross the stone bridge over the river – *the 'Bridge of Madoc', which gives Pontfadog its name.* Follow the road beneath woodland up to a junction. Here do a sharp U-turn and continue up the road, past cottages to minor crossroads. Take the rough lane ahead to begin a long steady climb through Coed Pen-craig. When it splits continue up the stony track ahead, later being joined by another forestry track. Eventually the track emerges from the wood – *with views across Cwm Gwryd* – then levels out – *with good views down to Llwynmawr and Glyn Ceiriog and to the distant Berwyns.* At a lane/track crossroads, turn LEFT and follow the enclosed track to a road. Turn LEFT along the road – *with distant views to Helsby and Frodsham and Beeston/Peckforton hills further south.*

2 At the junction by Plas Newydd, turn RIGHT – (For **Walk B** follow the road ahead down to point **3**) – then take the left fork. Shortly, the road is crossed by Offa's Dyke Path. Cross the stile on the left. Follow the stiled path beneath, then along the top of, the impressive dyke – *soon with a view across to Chirk, with its aqueduct/viaduct prominent* – later descending to an information board on a cross-track. A few yards to your right is a view across to Chirk castle. Continue up the narrow tree-lined stony track, past a stone enclosed well.

3 Where it joins a lane at the entrance to a house, go through a gate on the right. Go ahead across the field, over a stile, then descend into a side valley and up to a gate/telegraph pole. Here, turn RIGHT alongside the old wall – *with a good view across to Chirk castle, the Cheshire Plain and distant Pennines* – soon descending on a faint green track to pass between the wall and fence corner. Follow the track down to go through a large facing gate. Go down the field past a telegraph pole, then follow the fence on your right down to cross a stile in the bottom field corner. Turn LEFT down to another stile (now waymarked 'Ceiriog Valley Walk'), then follow the boundary on your right down towards cottages. After crossing a stile beneath outbuildings, go down the driveway to join a road by a large Nissan hut. *Further down the road is a property named after the Battle of Crogen in 1165 when Henry II's army was defeated by the Welsh, reputedly in this part of the Ceiriog valley.* Go up the high hedge-lined road, past a house. Later go down the right fork and follow the rougher lane to a cottage, then descend the shady road to the start.

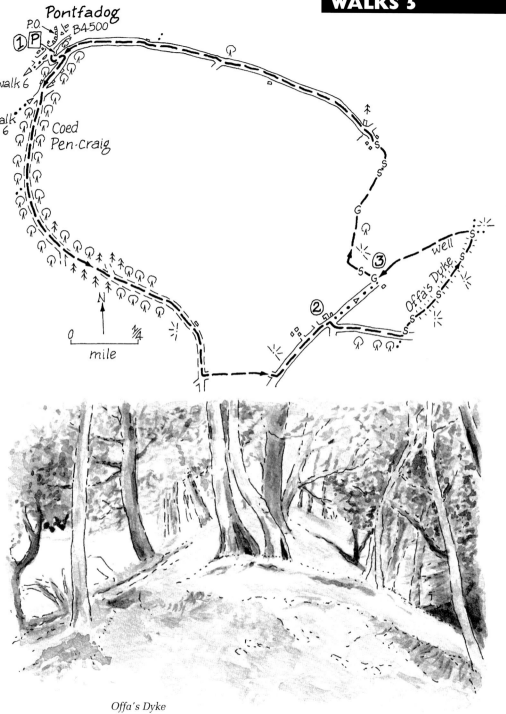

Offa's Dyke

7

WALK 6

ABOVE PONTFADOG

DESCRIPTION A 6 mile (**A**) or 4½ mile (**B**) walk, offering extensive ever-changing views, exploring the attractive hills and woodland near Pontfadog, using old tracks, bridleways and delightful flora rich hedge-lined quiet country lanes. The route climbs in stages to an upland road between the Ceiriog and Dee valleys, reaching a height of 1338 feet, before returning to the valley. Allow about 3½ hours.

START Car park, Pontfadog SJ 234380.

In 1893 the nearby Passenger Waiting Room was built for people travelling on the Glyn Valley Tramway (GVT), which stopped opposite. It began in 1873 as a narrow gauge gravity/horse-drawn tramway linking slate quarries at Glyn Ceiriog to the canal south of Chirk. In 1888, the Tramway was extended to Hendre dolerite quarry, rerouted to meet the Great Western railway at Chirk, and became steam powered. It ran mainly beside the road (B4500) past shops and cottages and was a daily feature of valley life. Until it closed in 1935, due to competition from road transport and the closure of quarries, the GVT was a lifeline for the valley, operating both freight and passenger services.

The main outward traffic was dolerite (granite) and slate, whilst a great variety of goods were brought back. The tramway eventually employed 4 locomotives, 14 coaches, 250 wagons and about 32 staff, with goods traffic peaking in 1919.

After closure the Waiting Room had a chequered history. In the 1950s, rate payments were collected here, earning it the nickname of 'Pontfadog town hall'! Eventually it was restored by the Glyn Valley Tramway Group, which aims to bring steam trains back to the valley. It is open on summer weekdays.

I Follow the lane adjoining the car park up to pass the bridge and cenotaph, then down past an information board about Ceiriog valley poets to the B5400. Cross to the pavement opposite and continue past the school, then St John's church. At the end of the pavement, continue along the road verge, soon reaching a crossroad. Here, turn RIGHT up the lane. Just beyond the garage of a house, keep ahead to follow a green hedge-lined track across the hillside – *with a good view overlooking Pontfadog and along the Ceiriog valley* – to eventually reach a lane by a farm. Turn LEFT, then at the junction, LEFT again on the waymarked Ceiriog Trail. Follow the lane up across the hillside.

2 At the outbuilding of a house, do a sharp U-turn to go through the higher of two gates. Keep ahead up to another gate at a good viewpoint. Continue with the bridleway, briefly tree-lined, soon crossing the open mid-slopes above a side valley, before rising steadily through trees, then open ground. Ignore a path going through a gate on your left, but keep straight ahead on a fainter path, soon improving and bending over a stream up to a gate. Go up the road. At the junction, turn LEFT along the road.

3 At the next junction, take the signposted path through a gate at Brynarddyn. (For **Walk B** follow the road on the left down to point **4**.) Bear RIGHT to pass round the rear of outbuildings to cross a stile. Now follow the stiled path along the edge of four fields, later rising to a road. *Here are new views north-east across to Ruabon Mountain and Cheshire.* Turn LEFT up the road – *later with good views west to the Berwyns.* At the next junction, at the highest point of the walk, take the signposted bridleway through a bridle gate on the left. Follow the gated bridleway along the edge of three fields then a hedge-lined section to a road. Follow it RIGHT, soon descending, then take a signposted bridleway through a bridle gate on the left. Go up the track. When it splits, keep ahead alongside the wall. Go past a gate in it to a bridle gate at the end of a plantation. The enclosed bridleway now crosses the hillside – *with a variety of wildflowers, blackthorn and rowan, and new views to Chirk Castle* – passing through two gates to reach a road. Turn RIGHT.

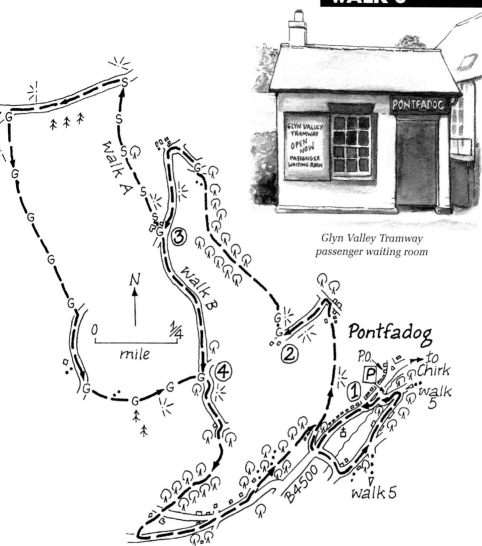

*Glyn Valley Tramway
passenger waiting room*

4 Continue along the road. When it bends left to Penybrongyll, keep ahead down a narrow tree-lined track, later descending more steeply through woodland. At a road, keep ahead down the access lane to nearby Bron gyll, then descend an old sunken track. At the next road, turn LEFT (Old Road) – *now joining the Ceiriog Valley Walk.* At the minor crossroads, keep ahead. Shortly, take a track angling off the road beneath the Old Rectory. Follow it past a stone building and up through the trees. At a finger post, take the waymarked Ceiriog Valley Walk below the track and follow the path across the wooded slope, later descending to pass above a house and bending down your outward route to the B5400. Take the road opposite to cross the river. At the junction, turn LEFT. Follow the road up past a house. At a crossroads, take the road angling down on the left, past cottages, then down through trees. At a junction, do a sharp U-turn down to cross the bridge over the river by the car park.

9

WALK 7
Y FOEL

DESCRIPTION A 8½ mile walk **(A)** exploring an upland area between the Dee and Ceiriog valleys. The route climbs steadily from Llangollen via Allt y Badi, an ancient highway linking the two valleys, now a stony track, then visits Y Foel (1712 feet), a wide heather hill offering panoramic views, now an Open Access area. After following a good path across its northern slopes, the route joins the waymarked section of the North Berwyn Way across attractive heather moorland, and on a long steady descent back to Llangollen. Allow about 4½ hours. The route can be shortened to a 5¼ mile walk **(B)** by utilising a quiet upland country road.

START Llangollen SJ 214420.

DIRECTIONS A large car park can be found in Market Street just off the main street.

1 Head south along the main street (Castle Street) to the traffic lights. Turn LEFT along the A5 (Berwyn Street), then cross the road to the nearby junction to go up Hill Street – signposted to Plas Newydd. Follow the road up to the entrance to Plas Newydd. Here go half-RIGHT across the junction along a pathway by Grange Road, then continue along the road. Shortly the road leaves houses and rises steadily. When it bends right take a signposted path over a stile to the left by a bench. Follow it down through trees, across a footbridge over the river, and on past a house to a lane. Turn RIGHT up the lane, which quickly becomes a narrow high hedge-lined track. This old highway (Allt y Badi) then becomes more stony and tree-lined, as it rises steadily, soon through mixed woodland. Eventually, it reaches more open country and becomes enclosed by walls. Shortly, the track levels out and reaches Pen-lan farm. Continue along the road to eventually reach crossroads by Bryn y Groes farm. Turn RIGHT, then RIGHT again at the next junction.

2 Soon take a signposted path over a stile on the left. (For **Walk B** simply continue along the road to point **5**.) Follow a green track up the long field edge to a stile. Go up the next field edge to a stile at a plantation corner. Go past the end of the plantation then cross a stile ahead to enter Open Access land. Go half-RIGHT to follow a waymarked path across the wide predominantly heather covered hillside of Y Foel, rising gently to reach a small cairned mound (the remains of Biddulph Tower) and a nearby trig point marking its summit. *Enjoy the panoramic all-round views: south across the Ceiriog valley; SE to the Shropshire hills; east to Chirk and across the Cheshire Plain and to the Pennines beyond; NE to Trevor Rocks, Ruabon Mountain; north to the Horseshoe Pass, Llantisilio Mountains, NW across Denbigh moors to Snowdonia; west to the Berwyn ridge.*

3 Return down the path and just before the stile turn LEFT to follow a faint green track up alongside the fence and on across the northern heather slopes of Y Foel. When the track angles away through heather, continue on a clear path beside the fence. It passes a gate in an adjoining fence, and continues on a gentle climb, passing a line of scattered stunted pine trees – *now with a view towards the Berwyns*. Eventually, at the fence corner, you reach a waymarked stile at a path junction. Cross the stile and follow the green track through the weather beaten pines, past another track coming in from the left at a waymark post. You are now joining the North Berwyn Way.

4 The track continues roughly north through heather and bilberry, offering extensive views. After crossing a stream, it bends right and splits. Take the waymarked left fork across the expansive heather moorland. At a cross-track, keep ahead, later running alongside a fence. After a stile/gate continue along the enclosed track to another stile. Later, after a gate, the track steadily descends to reach a road.

5 Go down the track opposite and follow this delightful bridleway on a long steady descent in stages towards Llangollen. After passing a ruin, the tree-lined bridleway descends more steeply – *with Llangollen briefly visible below* – and passes along the edge of woodland. At a bench and finger post, do a sharp U-turn down a path to cross a stile below. Follow the hedge down to a stile in it. Continue down the field edge – *with a*

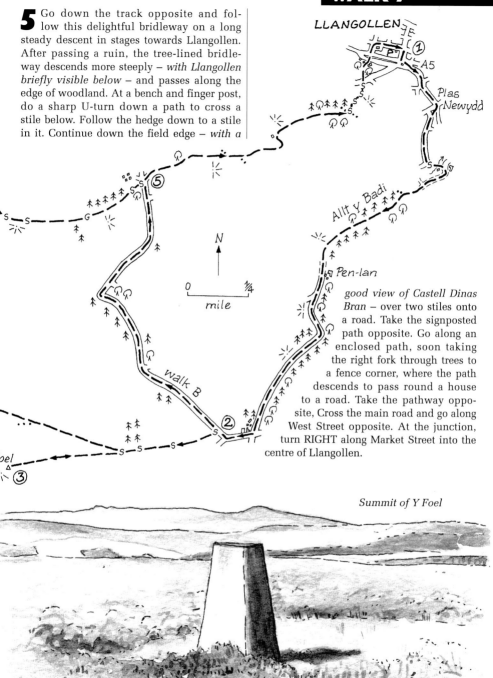

LLANGOLLEN

A5

Plas Newydd

⑤

Allt y Badi

Pen-lan

N

0 ¼

mile

walk B

②

Foel △ ③

good view of Castell Dinas Bran – over two stiles onto a road. Take the signposted path opposite. Go along an enclosed path, soon taking the right fork through trees to a fence corner, where the path descends to pass round a house to a road. Take the pathway opposite, Cross the main road and go along West Street opposite. At the junction, turn RIGHT along Market Street into the centre of Llangollen.

Summit of Y Foel

11

WALK 8
VIVOD MOUNTAIN

DESCRIPTION A 9 mile walk (**A**) to a high heather moorland ridge separating the Ceiriog and Dee valleys, offering panoramic views. The route climbs steadily from Glyn Ceiriog past the former Cambrian slate quarry, and across the western slopes of Y Foel to join a section of the North Berwyn Way across Vivod Mountain (1804 feet) and past Nantyr Forest. It then returns via the forest, upland road and a final delightful old sunken track. Allow about 5½ hours. A shorter 2½ mile walk (**B**) is included.
START Glyn Ceiriog SJ 202378.
DIRECTIONS The village lies on the B4500.

G lyn Ceiriog is the largest settlement in the valley and once a bustling slate village. After the 1870s life and work was dominated by the Cambrian and Wynne slate quarries just above the village, when production greatly expanded to meet increased demand for roofing slate and the creation of the Glyn Valley tramway provided transport out of the valley. Loaded wagons descended through the village to join the tramway. The Wynne quarry closed in 1923, while the Cambrian quarry, which employed 115 men in 1937, continued production until 1947.

The village was also an important centre for the fulling of woven wool to make flannel and blankets. Two mills in the village operated from the early 19thC until the mid-20thC. Glyn Ceiriog was a very religious and predominantly Welsh speaking community, with many local chapels and churches. It was a thriving community, with numerous social activities including eistedfodau, choirs, reading, horticultural and debating groups. The Glyn Valley Hotel – one of the stations on the horse tramway in 1874 – houses an interesting collection of Glyn Valley tramway photographs and artefacts.

From the crossroads, go along Quarry Road past the end of the Glyn Valley Hotel. The road soon rises past houses. Later, at a track junction, keep ahead along the access track to Chwarel up through the wood. When the track does a U-turn to Chwarel cross a stile ahead. Follow the path through the trees with glimpses of the huge Cambrian quarry to your right. The path later bends right and rises to a road. Turn RIGHT up the road past a house.

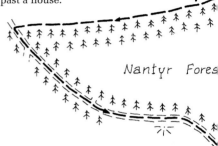

Nantyr Fores

2 Just before a junction take a track on the left by the entrance to Tan-y-foel. (For **Walk B**, at the junction, turn right along the stony track and resume text at point **4**.) Follow the hedge-lined stony track up to a road, then take a signposted path up a green track opposite to a stile/gate. Follow the fence on your left – *enjoying good views towards the Berwyns* – up to a gate at the plantation corner. Follow the path to a stile into Open Access land. Continue with the path across the heather/bracken covered western slopes of Y Foel then moorland to cross a stile at the corner of a small wood on a broad ridge – *with views to Llantisilio Mountains, Ruabon Mountain, Trevor Rocks, and Cheshire.* Follow the green track through the wind damaged pines.

3 Do a sharp U-turn LEFT to join the way-marked North Berwyn Way. It rises with the fence up the heather moorland and past a few stunted trees across the wide top of Vivod Mountain to cross a stile at its highest point. *Pause to enjoy the panoramic all-round views: from Shropshire hills to Snowdon, from the Berwyns to the Clwydian Hills.* Follow the path south through the heather, soon descending and bending with the fence towards the forest. It then continues alongside Nantyr Forest to eventually reach a road. Turn LEFT, over a cattle-grid and follow the track into the forest. When it splits keep ahead and follow the forestry track, past side tracks, then along the edge

Vivod
Mountain   walk 7

walk 7

Y Foel

N

0   ¼
  mile

P

walk 7

②

④ WALK B Glyn Ceiriog

quarry   quarry

tip

P   ①

B4500

B4579

ther 350 yards, take a narrow enclosed green track angling off on the right to join your outward route. Follow the track to the road. Turn LEFT then at the junction RIGHT.

4 Follow the hedge/tree lined stony track past a farm. It soon narrows and gently descends. When it forks to a gate, keep ahead on the delightful sunken hedge lined old track, little more than a path, soon descending, then widening and becoming a lane. Follow it down. When it bends left, keep ahead down the rough sunken track to join a lane by a house. Follow it down to crossroads in Glyn Ceiriog. Turn RIGHT and follow the road through the village past the Memorial

of upland pasture. After a dip, it becomes a rough road. At a junction, turn LEFT. Follow this attractive quiet country road along the southern edge of Nantyr Forest. After passing a large parking area it bends right. After a fur-

Institute – *opened in 1911 to serve the local community, its stained glass windows feature notable valley people.*

The Glyn Valley Hotel

13

WALK 9

MOEL FFERNA QUARRY

DESCRIPTION A fascinating and informative 7½ mile walk to a hillside slate quarry, which operated from the 1870s until 1960, once employing 200 men. The route rises across upland pasture, then follow the North Berwyn Way (NBW) to the Moel Fferna slate quarry (information boards). After a delightful section of old tramway, the NBW continues across heather moorland, reaching a height of 1706 feet before descending into Nant y Pandy valley, then through the narrow wooded gorge past a 19thC slate mill site (information boards). Allow about 5 hours.

START PO/stores, Glyndyfrdwy SJ 149427.

DIRECTIONS The PO/stores is at the junction of the A5 and the side road to Rhewl. Roadside parking further down or at nearby village hall.

1 Walk west on the pavement alongside the A5, then cross the road with care to go up the no through road opposite, At a junction continue up the road to take a signposted path on the right by a house. Go up the green track – *an early slab rock section can be slippy when wet* – to eventually reach a stile/gate, then follow it via further stiles/gates, later descending to a waymarked path junction by a red gate.

2 Turn LEFT up a green track to a stile/gate, then follow the stiled path along the edge of the next two fields. Go past sheepfolds to a stile in the corner. Follow the boundary on the right round to a stile/gate, then through the next field to another stile/gate. Follow the wall to cross a makeshift stile by a gate to join a green track just beyond by a gate at the forest corner. Here turn LEFT up the track and follow the waymarked NBW link path up across the expansive heather moorland to eventually reach a path junction at a second waymark post.

3 Continue ahead on the NBW path, past another waymarked junction, soon descending to a stream, then rising to join a green track which takes you to the quarry. The NBW path passes a large ruined building to reach three information boards at the top of an incline. Descend the incline, then continue on the delightful stiled/gated former tramway to a fence corner. The NBW path rises through heather, soon angling away from the fence across the heather moorland, then continues south alongside a fence, past a small tip, and up to join the ridge track. Turn LEFT.

4 Follow the rough track past Nantyr Forest to a road. Turn LEFT along the road, soon descending. (An option is to follow the scenic road down above the valley, then turn sharp left down a stony track to point **5**.) Shortly, take the NBW footpath on the left down the predominantly heather/bilberry covered hillside, later continuing above the stream to emerge onto a track. Go down the former tramway and on past two houses. At a junction keep ahead, past a signposted bridleway to reach a finger post.

5 Take the path signposted Nant y Pandy, soon crossing a footbridge, where a reservoir once provided power for the Nant y Pandy mill. The path descends past small waterfalls, then passes through the former Nant y Pandy mill site. At a signposted path junction, continue ahead down through the narrow wooded valley to cross a footbridge by Pandy Cottages. Follow the green track past a house and on to reach the Village Hall.

WALK 10

MOEL FFERNA

DESCRIPTION A 7½ mile (**A**) or a more demanding 8¾ mile (**B**) walk that rises in stages from the Dee Valley across upland pasture and expansive moorland to Moel Fferna (2066 feet) for panoramic views. **Walk A** continues along the moorland ridge. **Walk B** soon descends to follow the NBW via Moel Fferna quarry, later rejoining **Walk A** on the ridge, then descending

14

into Nant y Pandy valley. Allow about 5 hours.
START As **Walk 9**

1–2 Follow instructions in paragraphs 1 and 2 of **Walk 9**.

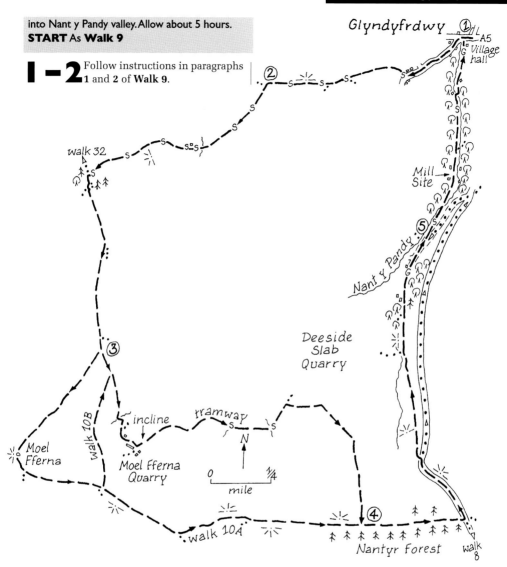

3 Bear RIGHT and follow the rough track up the heather hillside to reach two small stone summit shelters on Moel Fferna. Now follow a peaty path south east to the join a track at the NBW stile. Follow it east alongside the ridge fence, soon descending to a NBW waymark post beyond a stile. (For **Walk B**, follow the waymarked path down through heather to a waymarked path junction. Follow the NBW right to the quarry,

down the incline, along the tramway, and up to rejoin the ridge path – see **Walk 9** for more details.) For **Walk A** continue with the track, soon bending away from the fence and meandering across the expansive heather moorland later rejoining the fence then descending to join **Walk 9** at point **4**.

4 Follow instructions in paragraphs **4** and **5** of **Walk 9**.

15

WALK 11

COED COLLFRYN

DESCRIPTION A 5 mile (**A**) walk exploring the attractive countryside between Glyn Ceiriog and Dolywern. After following a quiet country lane up into open country, the route crosses delightful upland pasture (1213 feet) offering extensive views, before descending and continuing to Coed Collfryn and Dolywern. It then returns along a section of the Ceiriog Valley Way. Allow about 3 hours. A shorter 3 mile walk (**B**) is included.
START Glyn Valley Hotel, Glyn Ceiriog SJ 202378

1 Go down the B4579 (Selatyn/Oswestry) past the Post Office. After crossing the river, take the side road on the right. After passing the trout farm, the road rises steadily along the wooded edge of the Ceiriog valley. At Pant Farm, take a signposted path along a track on the left. On the bend by two corrugated sheds, cross a stile on the left.

2 Go up the field edge to cross another stile. Turn LEFT, then angle up to continue near a higher fence. After a stile in the corner, bear RIGHT up through gorse and on to a waymark post. Bear LEFT across upland pasture, past another waymark post – *enjoying extensive views* – to cross the wall corner ahead by gorse. Descend with the boundary on your right. At the bottom, turn RIGHT down between boundaries, soon joining a green track, which steadily descends to a stile/gate. Shortly, when it bends into a field, keep ahead with the avenue of trees to a stile. Follow the boundary on your right down to cross two stiles to reach a road by a bungalow. (For **Walk B** follow the road down to Glyn Ceiriog.)

3 Take the signposted path from the end of Hillside opposite down to a stile, then angle LEFT down the steep field, then go along the slope to a waymarked gate. Descend to a green track, then a gate below by the large house. Descend steps, then turn RIGHT along a rough green track, through

two gates and on along the top of a steep field. When it ends follow the boundary on the left through two fields to a stile. Go across the top of the next long field to cross a hidden stile in a side valley, then a stream. Follow the path to a stile into Coed Collfryn. Continue up to a crossroad of paths. Turn LEFT down to a kissing gate out of the wood. Continue to a stile onto a road in Dolywern. Turn LEFT.

4 At the junction go along the road ahead, over the river, then take an old track (Glan-y-Wern Hill) up to Old Road. Follow it LEFT, then take a signposted path on the right to a stile between houses. Follow the waymarked stiled Ceiriog Valley Way up through mixed woodland, a field edge, and an enclosed path to cross a stile on the left opposite a house into a field. Go along the tree boundary to cross a stile in it. Continue below the boundary to a stile. Later angle down to pass beneath Scots pines and on between derelict buildings. Go down the lane. On the bend take the signposted path through a gate ahead, past the house and through a gate at the end of stables. Descend the waymarked path to cross a footbridge and stile. Descend to a tree boundary and follow it along the field. At its end go half-LEFT down to a lane. Follow it RIGHT. At the second junction, turn LEFT to reach the main road at Glyn Ceiriog. Cross to the house opposite and follow the path near the river past various properties, then go up the road past the Post Office to the start.

WALK 12

PANDY TRAMWAY

DESCRIPTION This 6 mile walk follows the Ceiriog Valley Way to Pandy, then the delightful Glyn Valley tramway owned by the National Trust. It continues with the Ceiriog Trail up the attractive part wooded valley, before returning down a quiet upland country road. Allow about 4 hours. The route can easily be extended to 6¾ or 8¾ mile walks when combined with **Walk 11** from point **2** via the link bridleway shown. The tramway can also be accessed from

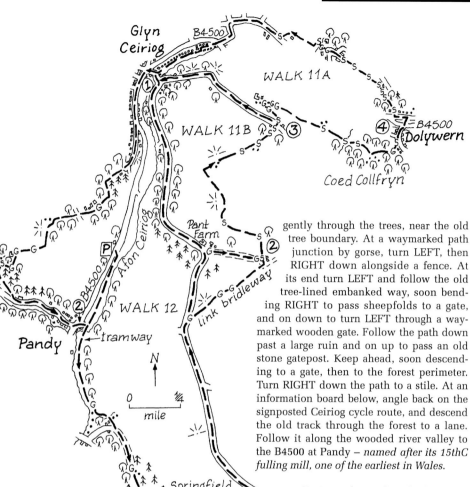

gently through the trees, near the old tree boundary. At a waymarked path junction by gorse, turn LEFT, then RIGHT down alongside a fence. At its end turn LEFT and follow the old tree-lined embanked way, soon bending RIGHT to pass sheepfolds to a gate, and on down to turn LEFT through a waymarked wooden gate. Follow the path down past a large ruin and on up to pass an old stone gatepost. Keep ahead, soon descending to a gate, then to the forest perimeter. Turn RIGHT down the path to a stile. At an information board below, angle back on the signposted Ceiriog cycle route, and descend the old track through the forest to a lane. Follow it along the wooded river valley to the B4500 at Pandy – *named after its 15thC fulling mill, one of the earliest in Wales.*

2 Cross the road to the bus shelter then follow Maes-y-Pannwr down past houses to the Glyn Valley tramway. Follow it RIGHT past an information board, over the river and on beneath the wooded slopes. Later take a signposted path through a gate on the left into Open Access land. Follow the path, soon rising across the bracken slope and continuing alongside a wood, past a waymarked side path to join a lane. Follow it up the valley, later becoming a track. Keep with the left fork to climb steadily up past part felled Springfield Wood to eventually reach a road. Follow it LEFT. At a junction, keep ahead and follow the quiet country road down to Glyn Ceiriog.

a small parking area on the B4500 by Coed-y-Glyn Uchaf for a simple riverside stroll.
START As **Walk 11.**

I Follow the B4500 south towards Pandy. Shortly take a road on the right signposted to Nantyr. When it bends sharp right, keep ahead past a wooden cottage to follow a path up through mixed woodland to a gate. Continue ahead past farm buildings, then follow the tree boundary on the right to cross a lane. The waymarked path rises

WALK 13

SPRINGFIELD WOOD

DESCRIPTION A 4½ mile walk (**A**) or 3 mile walk (**B**) exploring different scenic valleys, with good views. The route ascends an attractive side valley, reaching a height of 1410 feet. **Walk B** returns along upland tracks, then an old sunken track. **Walk A** continues across upland pasture, then descends past Springfield Wood, before returning on the Ceiriog Valley Way. Allow about 3 and 2 hours respectively.
START Lay-by near Pontricket Farm SJ 186344
DIRECTIONS The lay-by adjoins the B4500 1¼ miles south of Pandy, just before Pontricket Farm.

Continue to the entrance to Pontricket farm, then take a lane angling down to cross a bridge over the river. At its end go along the track ahead past a cottage to cross a stile above the track. Go up the long field and through a waymarked wooden gate near its top left-hand corner. Continue by the nearby stream, soon crossing it. Go up the field edge initially near another stream to go through a gate ahead. Turn RIGHT on the waymarked path up a green track. It rises steadily, crosses a stream and continues up the valley, later levelling out across rough upland pasture, to reach a stile/gate at the bend of a green track. (For **Walk B** turn right along the gated track, later descending to a track junction. Follow the track ahead down past a farm to a lane. Go down its right fork and through a facing gate. Descend the track to join your outward route.)

2 Go ahead along the track to go through a gate by signs. Angle LEFT to follow a green track across the field to a gate. Continue with the fenced track, later descending. Just before the road, turn LEFT to follow another track down past part felled Springfield Wood. Later it becomes a rough lane which descends past a cottage to a junction. Take the signposted path through a gate ahead to pass Clochd y'r Bont and on to a stile. Follow the former tramway through

the trees, then leave it to rise away from the river. Follow the waymarked path through woodland passing beneath the former Hendre dolerite quarry (1873-1950), later rising along the wood edge to pass between a house and outbuildings. Follow its access track down to a cottage to join your outward route.

WALK 14

PEN-Y-GWELY

DESCRIPTION An 8¼ mile (**A**) walk across expansive upland pasture and rolling hills on a network of delightful green tracks, offering extensive views. After an initial climb from the Ceiriog valley, the route continues across an upland plateau, descends to Pen-y gwely reservoir, then follows the Ceiriog Trail to cross the broad top of Pen y Gwely (1443 feet), before returning down an attractive valley. Allow about 5 hours. The route also includes alternative 6¾ mile (**B**), 4 mile (**C**), or 3 mile (**D**) walks.
START As **Walk 13**.

I Continue to the entrance to Pontricket farm, then take a lane angling down to cross a bridge over the river. At its end go along the track ahead past a cottage, then follow the initially tree-lined sunken track up to a gate. Go up the lane, then take its left fork up to a gate. Continue past the farm up across the head of the valley to where it splits. (For **Walk D**, go up its left fork to a gate, afterwards levelling out. After two further gates cross a stile on its bend to rejoin the main route.)

3 Continue down the forestry track and on past the attractive Pen-y-Gwely reservoir. When opposite the dam, turn sharp RIGHT up a green track to a gate above a farm. Continue alongside the fence, soon descending to a gate and through the forest edge. After another gate, do a sharp U-turn to the gate below and follow the track down to a road. Go up the road and on past a bungalow, then turn LEFT down the access lane to Bwlchydonge. Go through the lower of two gates by the house. Go down the green track, over a stream, and up to a gate. Continue up the track alongside the conifer, then fence boundary to go through a gate. Go along the field edge to a gateway and a track junction.

4 Continue ahead with the track, soon rising steadily to a gate, then its highest point. The track now begins a long steady descent. After a gate, turn LEFT up another track, later passing a large corrugated building and a plantation to a go through a gate at its far corner. Continue west alongside the fence across Pen y Gwely – *soon with panoramic views unfolding* – through another gate and on to a signposted bridleway (**Walk C**).

5 Continue ahead with the fence, through a gateway, and on to go through a gate in the corner by signs. Go along the green track. On the bend cross a stile, then head half-LEFT across rough upland pasture, soon descending to join a green track. Follow it down into the attractive valley, later crossing a stream and continuing down to eventually go through a waymarked gate. Go down the field, soon near the stream, to cross another stream at the bottom. Bear RIGHT to a waymarked wooden gate. Go down the middle of the long field to a stile to join your outward route.

2 Go up its right fork. Follow the delightful green track through three gates to reach a signposted bridleway/path junction. (For **Walk C** follow the bridleway left to a gate, and up to go through another gate. Turn left and resume text at point **5**.) Keep ahead with the green track across upland pasture through three gates to enter an area of young forest. Go along the forestry track. (Shortly, for **Walk B** take the green track on the left along the top edge of the forest, then on between tree and fence boundaries to a track junction at a facing gate. Turn sharp left and resume text at point **4**.)

CEFN-HIR-FYNYDD

DESCRIPTION A delightful 4¾ mile walk exploring the unspoilt valley and hills just south of Llanarmon. The route follows a bridleway up to the head of an attractive side valley (**route A**), an area of Open Access, or via two tops (1378 feet) offering extensive views (**route B**). It then follows a splendid section of the Upper Ceiriog Trail across Cefn-Hir-fynydd (1509 feet) – offering great views – before returning by quiet country road. Allow about 3 hours.
START Llanarmon Dyffryn Ceiriog SJ 157328.

Llanarmon Dyffryn Ceiriog stands at a key crossing point of the Ceiriog river used by Iron Age settlers, Romans, then monks from Valle Crucis Abbey. In later centuries Llanarmon developed as an important stopping place for drovers on their way to markets in England. It takes its name from the religious site dedicated to St Garmon, a French Bishop, established here in the 5thC. By the churchyard gate of the current Victorian church is said to be the original preaching mound. There are yew trees over 1000 years old. The renowned 19thC Welsh poet John 'Ceiriog' Hughes was born here.

I Take the road signposted to Llanrhaeadr, soon passing the school and leaving the village. Shortly, take a signposted path through a gate on the left, past a house to another gate. Now follow a delightful bridleway up the valley and beneath the bracken slopes of Pen y Glog, later rising into a side valley. At a small rise ignore the level green way ahead, but bear LEFT up a path, soon bending and levelling out to reach a bracken covered low embanked field boundary. (For **route B** head up the slope to a small rocky top at the western end of the ridge, then follow the fence east to another small top, before descending to a small gate.) For **route A**, pass through the boundary, and after 75 yards, leave the path and head half-LEFT up the slope to the left of a small rocky knoll, where you join

a path which takes you to a small gate. Go along the edge of a reedy area to a stile in the fence. Keep ahead to pass through a reedy area and on up to a gate above onto a track.

2 Turn RIGHT and follow the gated track to and across the broad grassy ridge of Cefn-Hir-fynydd – *enjoying extensive views, especially west to the Berwyns* – later descending to a road. Follow it RIGHT down to Llanarmon.

WALK 16

BWLCH-ADWY-WYNT

DESCRIPTION An 8 mile (**A**) or 6 mile (**B**) walk of great variety, with extensive views. After climbing a quiet country road the route follows a delightful section of the Upper Ceiriog Trail across Cefn-Hir-Fynydd (1509 feet), before continuing by track, attractive country lanes, and sunken green lane down into the Ceiriog valley. It then returns on a section of the Ceiriog Valley Walk (CVW) through fields and woodland. Allow about 4½ hours.
START Llanarmon Dyffryn Ceiriog SJ 157328.

a steady descent. At a junction keep ahead, then go through the facing gate. (The one on the left offers another option via a house and stables). Go down the narrow track, soon sunken and tree-lined.

3 Later go through a waymarked gate on the left to join the Ceiriog Valley Walk. After a stile, follow the hedge on your left to another stile. Follow the path to a stile by a stream. Continue on the waymarked permissive path/CVW alongside the fence to a gate and on beneath slopes grazed by horses to a lane. (If the permissive path is closed, go to a nearby stile and head up to the white house above. Turn right and follow the rough lane down.) Follow the attractive lane to a road by the bridge over the river. Go along the track opposite past a farm. After a gate continue up the rough lane, then follow the waymarked CVW through a gate on the right.

4 Go across the field then follow the path through mixed woodland and along the wood edge by a fence to a gate at its corner. Keep ahead alongside the fence, soon following a track past a house. When it bends left keep ahead across reedy ground to cross a stile. Go through the adjoining gate and angle across the field up to another stile. Go across the next field and down to a gate. Follow the path past a large stone barn and on to reach the road by an information board about proposals to flood the valley. Follow the road down to past St Garmon's church into Llanarmon.

1 Take the road signposted to Llanrhaeadr, soon leaving the village. It continues along the valley, then rises steadily south west. Just before a road junction, go through a gate on the left. Now follow a gated green track up the hillside and across the wide grassy ridge of Cefn-Hir-fynydd – *enjoying extensive changing views*. Later the track meanders across more open tussocky ground, soon descending to a gate, then rising again to pass a waymarked gate on the left.

2 Continue along the track, soon descending to a crossroads of tracks. (For **Walk B**, turn left down the old track to a road. Go through the gate opposite and follow the hedge lined track down the hillside, later passing a waymarked gate (another less walked option), narrowing then becoming a rough lane. Go through a gate on the left opposite a waymark post then resume text at point **4**.) For **Walk A** follow the delightful track ahead for ½ mile to a road at Bwlch-adwy-wynt. Follow it RIGHT. At the junction, turn LEFT, then RIGHT up the narrow road (Upper Ceiriog Trail). Shortly, it begins

WALK 17

BRYN DDU

DESCRIPTION A 4¼ mile walk along the wooded edge of the valley, later following a bridleway up into open country to the moorland edge of Bryn Ddu (1640 feet), before returning down a section of the Upper Ceiriog Trail. Allow about 3 hours.
START Llanarmon Dyffryn Ceiriog SJ 157328.

1 Follow the B4500 back over the river. On the bend go up the lane ahead. After it bends left, go through a gate on the left and across the steep slope to a stile into Coed Cochion. Follow the path down through the trees, then continue with a green gated track along the bottom edge of deciduous woodland, later alongside a fence in a more open aspect. After a gate above a large barn, keep ahead to go through a waymarked facing gate. Descend to a track. Follow the gated track up the side valley and into open country to eventually go through a gate beyond a large barn. Turn RIGHT along the field edge to a waymarked corner and up to go through a wooden gate in the boundary.

2 Angle LEFT across the field to pass a gated fence corner and continue below the fence to a gate ahead and along the track After another gate the track descends. Turn LEFT through a gate opposite a corrugated barn. Descend to cross the stream, go up the slope, then through reeds to pass to the left of the gated fence corner ahead. Work your way up through reeds, following the fence on your right, to an old gate. Go up the steep field to another gate into Open Access land. Just beyond, turn RIGHT and follow a track, then path across reedy/heather moorland. At a green cross-track by a TV aerial, follow it LEFT, later on its right fork to reach a track by a forest. Go through the nearby gate and follow the track, then lane down to the B4500 at Llanarmon.

WALK 18

CEIRIOG GORGE

DESCRIPTION A 9 mile (**A**) or 8½ mile (**B**) walk exploring Open Access land at the remote upper reaches of the Afon Ceiriog, featuring its narrow rocky gorge and delightful waterfalls. Preferred **Route A** follows an improving path across the upper slopes with good views of the waterfalls. **Route B** follows the waymarked footpath across moorland (1574 feet). **Route C** follows the river up through the gorge, later tough underfoot. After open and forest tracks, the route follows a bridleway across moorland later with a choice of routes, before a long steady descent on the Upper Ceiriog Trail. For experienced walkers and avoid in poor visibility. Allow about 5½ hours.
START Llanarmon Dyffryn Ceiriog SJ 157328.

1 From the village centre take the No Through road signposted to Swch-cae-rhiw along the Ceiriog valley. (After 1¾ miles, if seeking relief from tarmac, turn RIGHT along a lane by an old chapel, over the river and on between a house and a converted barn. Go through a gate ahead on the waymarked path. Follow the gated stony track to its end, Bear LEFT to continue near the fence, then go across the mid-slopes and on to a gate in the wall. Go along the next field to cross a footbridge over the river to rejoin the road above.) At the road end, follow the signposted path down the track, over the river, up the left fork past Swch-cae-rhiw. Continue up to a stile, then up past pines to a gate into Open Access land – *with a good view into the Ceiriog gorge.*

2 Continue up the green track.

Route C: after 40 yards, angle down to join a path overlooking the river. Follow it to a fence with a waterfall ahead. Climb up alongside the fence, then follow it across the undulating tussocky slope to eventually reach level ground beyond the final waterfall. Bear left to join route **A**.
Route B: at the top of the track, follow the waymarked path across moorland, later descending through heather into the wide

junction – *with views to Cheshire and distant Pennines.* (For **Walk B**, turn right up the path to a heather track, then cross a stile beyond. Continue with the path, soon following a fence across the moorland of Bryn Ddu, to join **Walk A** at a track by a gate at a forest corner.)

flat upland valley to point **3**.

Route A: near the top of the track at a metal waterbut, angle up to the top of the nearby crag. As the ground begins to descend towards the gorge bear LEFT along a faint path. After a small crag, follow an improving path north across the upper slopes, soon enjoying views of the waterfalls below. As it nears the upper falls, the path bends away across tussocky ground into a wide flat upland valley. It continues parallel with the meandering infant Ceiriog below, then beneath heather to meet the descending footpath (**B**).

3 Follow the path to cross the Afon Ceiriog and a stile ahead. Follow the path to a green track. Follow it RIGHT, soon joined by another, to a stile into a forest. Keep with the green track to join a wider forestry track. Later as the track bends up left, angle through adjoining bracken to pass a nearby fence compound, then continue along a green track. Just before it rejoins the forestry track, turn RIGHT to a waymark post below. Follow the bridleway to a gate and across the bilberry/bracken slope, soon rising then contouring across the moorland. Shortly, take the right fork, soon beginning a long steady climb to eventually reach a waymarked bridleway/path

4 For **Route A.** Keep ahead with the bridleway down to join another track to go through a gate. Follow the old green track to another gate onto a more defined track (Upper Ceiriog Way). Follow it RIGHT down to cross a stream and up across the moorland to a gate at the forest corner, being joined by **Walk B**. After another gate simply follow the track, then lane down to the B4500 at Llanarmon.

23

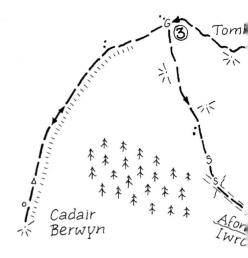

WALK 19

TOMLE & CADAIR BERWYN

DESCRIPTION A 9¼ mile (**A**) or 7 mile (**B**) walk for experienced walkers accessing the Berwyn ridge from the east along an undulating moorland ridge, now Open Access land. The route climbs steadily from the valley up to join the moorland ridge, which it follows west on a surprisingly good path across Foel Wen to reach Tomle (2433 feet), then a bwlch. From here, **Walk A** makes the short climb onto the ridge for a there and back walk to the two peaks of Cadair Berwyn (2722 feet). The route then descends into Cwm Iwrch and returns along the attractive valley via track and quiet country road. Allow about 5½ hours for the full walk. *Avoid in poor visibility.*

START Cwm Maen Gwynedd SJ 119306.

DIRECTIONS From Llanarmon Dyffryn Ceiriog, take the road signposted to Llanrhaeadr-ym-Mochnant. After about 2 miles, at a junction, keep straight ahead on a narrow road signposted to Maen Gwynedd, soon on a long descent to a junction. Follow the road past an outdoor education centre. Shortly a narrow road joins from the left – this is the one you should take. First, go to another nearby junction by a telephone box, turn round and take the narrow road down to find parking for two or three cars just before the bridge over the river.

1 Return up the road. At the junction continue ahead. At the next junction, turn RIGHT past the telephone box and the farm. Follow the road up to another farm. Go through the farmyard and continue up the lane, soon becoming a track. On the bend go through the right of two facing gates on a waymarked Tir Gofal path. Go up the field and through a waymarked gate at the top. Go half-RIGHT past Scots pines, then follow an old sunken green track up to a gate at a forest corner. Now bear LEFT up across upland pasture, gradually moving away from the fence. Go past the higher of two old fence posts, angling up the hillside – *with views to*

Cadair Berwyn – soon on a faint green track. After a gate, continue up the rough track, then follow the line of the reedy track across the hillside – *with new views across to Foel Wen.* Shortly, follow the rough track bending right up the hillside to moorland peaty edges to cross a stile in a fence. Work your way up onto the craggy ridge of Cerrig Geneugiaid just ahead – *with good views north.*

2 Head west to another rocky top, then descend to the fence below to join a path. Continue beside the fence, soon rising steadily to cross the wide moorland ridge – *ahead is Cadair Bronwen, with views towards Snowdonia.* The path rises again and crosses Foel Wen, before descending, then beginning a long steady climb with the fence to a tiny cairn on the top of Tomle – *offering extensive all-round views.* Continue with the fence across level but peaty ground to reach a gate in the fence junction at a bwlch beneath the Berwyn ridge – *with a view across to the the cairned top of Cadair Bronwen.* Your return path now descends LEFT. For **Walk A**, cross the facing fence and follow a path up the left hand side of the fence onto the Berwyn ridge. Follow it to the two tops of Cadair Berwyn, then retrace your steps.

3 Follow a path on a long steady descent into Cwm Iwrch, later taking the left fork to cross a ladder-stile. Go half-LEFT down the field to another ladder-stile onto a track. Follow it down the valley. After passing through two gates, the track passes a small

24

plantation, through another gate at its end. Later the track becomes hedged/tree lined as it continues along the valley then becomes a road. Follow the road through the more gentle arable Cwm Maen Gwynedd past farms back to the start.

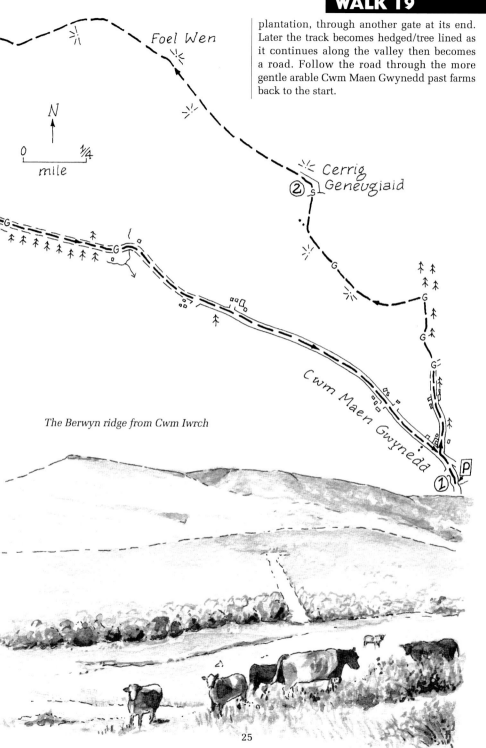

The Berwyn ridge from Cwm Iwrch

WALK 20

PISTYLL RHAEADR

DESCRIPTION Pistyll Rhaeadr, at 240 feet, is the longest waterfall in England and Wales. At Tan-y-Pistyll, there is a signposted walk to the base of the waterfall, then up to its top and back. This more rewarding 3 mile walk (**A**) first explores an attractive side valley offering good views of the waterfall and Cadair Berwyn, and extends to delightful small waterfalls. It returns down the valley to visit both the top and foot of Pistyll Rhaeadr. Allow about 2 hours. The route includes alternative 2½ mile (**B**) or 1¼ mile (**C**) walks which omit the climb to the top of the waterfall.
START Car park, Pistyll Rhaeadr SJ 076294.
DIRECTIONS From the centre of Llanrhaeadr-ym-Mochnant, take the single track road signposted to the waterfall. Follow it for 3¾ miles to find riverside parking areas just before its end, where there is also a pay and display car park by Tan-y-pistyll cafe and toilets.

1 Go back up the road, soon levelling out. After a further 300 yards, cross a stile up on the left into Open Access land. Follow the delightful green track back across the gorse and heather covered hillside, soon rising and bending into the side valley – *enjoying good views of Pistyll Rhaeadr* – to where it splits. (For **Walk C**, take the left fork, soon descending to cross a stile and stream. Follow the track above back down the valley. After a kissing gate follow a woodland path to Pistyll Rhaeadr, returning via Tan-y-Pistyll cafe.) For **Walks A** and **B** go up the right fork, with Cadair Berwyn on the skyline ahead, to a stile. Continue with the track up the eastern side of the valley to cross another stile.

2 Here follow the fence down into the valley, later moving away from it to follow a path through bracken, then rejoining it. Cross the Nant y Llyn just upstream of the fence, then follow the fence up to an adjoining fence/gate before sheepfolds (point **3**). Pass to the right of the sheepfolds and follow the stream up to where it meets another. Turn LEFT up the stream to two small waterfalls. Retrace your steps to pass the sheepfolds.

3 Cross the fence, go through the adjoining gateway and head south along the valley on a path then green track. Shortly, cross a stile at a boundary corner. Follow the fence down to rejoin the green track, which descends to the bend of another track. (For **Walk B** keep ahead down the track. After a kissing gate follow a woodland path to Pistyll Rhaeadr, returning via Tan-y-Pistyll cafe.) For **Walk A** bear RIGHT up the track, past a way-marked path (point **4** – your return route). At another waymark post turn LEFT and follow the path down through a kissing gate then trees to reach the top of the waterfall. Return to the track and follow it back down.

4 Shortly, take a waymarked path on the right, jig-zagging down into the valley. After a kissing gate follow the woodland path to a footbridge over the river beneath the impressive waterfall. Follow a riverside path to Tan-y-Pistyll cafe, then the road back to the start.

WALK 21

CADAIR BERWYN & PISTYLL RHAEADR

DESCRIPTION A 6 mile walk for experienced walkers offering the shortest and most attractive climb to Cadair Berwyn, combined with a visit to the longest waterfall in England and Wales. The route follows a delightful green track on a steady climb up an attractive side valley, then a path past Llyn Lluncaws, before a final climb to Moel Sych. After following the ridge to Cadair Berwyn (2722 feet) and returning to Moel Sych, the route follow a good path down open slopes to Pistyll Rhaeadr. Allow about 4 hours. Avoid in poor visibility.
START Car park, Pistyll Rhaeadr SJ 076294.

1 Follow the main instructions in paragraph **1** of **Walk 20**.

2 Continue up the valley, later crossing the Nant y Llyn. A waymarked permissive path now continues up to Llyn Lluncaws, rises more steeply, then climbs along the edge overlooking the lake – take care – to eventually reach the main ridge just below the top of Moel Sych. Follow the path along the ridge up to a ladder-stile to reach the craggy top of Cadair Berwyn for panoramic views from Snowdon to Cheshire. Continue north past the stone shelter, down past a small pool and up to the trig point. Return to the ladder-stile and follow the ridge back towards Moel Sych.

3 After a peaty flattish section, take a path angling away from the edge to follow the nearby fence up to a ladder-stile on the wide flat top of Moel Sych, with a cairn just beyond. Don't cross the ladder-stile, but turn LEFT to follow a path heading south down beside the fence – *enjoying extensive views*. After crossing a flat peaty area, the path rises with the fence, before beginning a long steady descent to a ladder-stile. Continue with the path down the hillside, later descending towards Cwm Rhaeadr to eventually reach a waymark post on a green track. (The waymarked path ahead leads down to the top of the waterfall – a there and back option.) Turn LEFT along the track, soon descending into the side valley.

4 Follow instructions in paragraph **4** of **Walk 20** to descend to the waterfall.

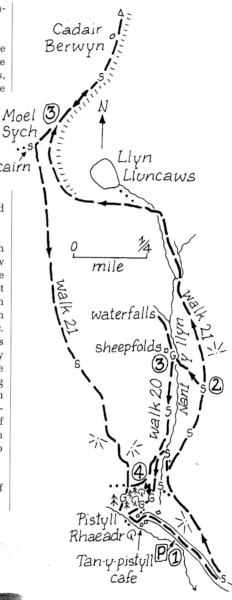

Llyn Lluncaws

27

Y CLOGYDD & PISTYLL RHAEADR

DESCRIPTION An 8¾ mile (**A**) or 7¾ mile (**B**) walk for experienced walkers from the Tanat valley across hills to Pistyll Rhaeadr, the highest waterfall in England and Wales. The route passes beneath Craig Rhiwarth into the Sebon valley, then climbs steeply to a bwlch (1738 feet). It continues along an upland track, descends to cross the Afon Disgynfa, then continues down to Pistyll Rhaeadr and Tan-y-Pistyll cafe. After climbing out of the valley, **Route B** returns down your outward bridleway, while **Route A** extends across wilder Open Access land, before descending into the Sebon valley. Both routes combine for a delightful riverside finish. Allow about 6 hours. The route can be shortened to a 5½ mile walk (**C**) at point **3**. Avoid in poor visibility.
START Llangynog car park SJ 054262
DIRECTIONS Llangynog lies on the B4391. Its car park is in the village centre.

L langynog, now a small farming community, nestles beneath steep mountains bearing the scars of its industrial past. The village, standing on an ancient drovers route, grew rapidly from the early 18thC when it became a major lead mining area, once employing 2000 men. Slate and granite were also quarried until the middle of the last century. On the summit of Craig Rhiwarth – said to be the haunt of fairies – is an Iron Age hillfort.

I From the car park turn RIGHT. Go over the river, then take the side road. At the junction turn RIGHT and follow the road beneath Craig Rhiwarth, then take a signposted bridleway on the left. It soon rises across the slate debris/bracken covered hillside to a gate, then up through oak woodland. After emerging onto the hillside it bends north to meet a track at a stile/gate.

2 Cross the stile into Open Access land and go along the green track. Shortly, take the waymarked bridleway on the right to cross

Nant Sebon and a stile. Go up the slope to a stile/gate, then follow a bridleway north up the valley edge. After another stile, turn RIGHT to follow the waymarked bridleway up the steep hillside. Eventually it levels out, beneath the small southern ridge of Y Clogydd. Here the bridleway bears RIGHT across reedy ground. (Another option is via the inauspicious top of Y Clogydd for all-round views, as shown.) After a stile/gate keep ahead.

3 After about 250 yards, when the bridleway angles down to a waymark post, keep ahead. (For **Walk C** then turn LEFT to join the return route of **Walk A**.) Continue through bracken then reeds to reach the bend of a track ahead. Go up the track and along Craig y Mwn, later descending to cross a stream, then continue across upland pasture. Go past a gate in a fence corner above a ravine. At the next corner go half-RIGHT with the fence to join a path a few yards from it. Soon take the right fork to begin a long steady descent across the hillside to go through a gate by conifers above the Afon Disgynfa. Bear sharp RIGHT down a path. Just before it enters bracken, descend to cross the river and a fence above. Go up through bracken to join a good cross-path. Follow it RIGHT, later passing a waymark post, where a path descends to the top of Pistyll Rhaeadr (a there and back option). The stony track soon descends. Shortly, take a waymarked path on the right, jig-zagging down into the valley. After a kissing gate follow the woodland path to a footbridge over the river beneath the impressive waterfall.

4 Cross the footbridge and follow the path through the wood edge and across the undulating bracken slope to cross a stream and stile, then another stile above. Follow the level path alongside the fence and on through old workings. *The upper slopes of Craig y Mwn have been mined for lead from the 17thC until the early 20thC.* At a track, turn LEFT for a few yards, then continue with the path past a ruin to a waymark post. Turn RIGHT and follow the bridleway up the hillside, soon near the fence to reach a track. Go up the track, soon bending west above a side valley. On the next bend keep ahead up the waymarked bridleway to a familiar waymark post. (For **Walk B** follow your outward route down to point **7**.)

5 Go straight ahead to cross your outward route, and on up the slope ahead. At the fence on the skyline, follow it RIGHT to go through a gate in the corner. Bear LEFT along a path parallel with the fence. After 120 yards, at stones, just before it descends, bear RIGHT across high ground, then descend to cross a fence. Go ahead for about 100 yards, then go half-LEFT to join an improving old reedy track, which then gently descends, later near a fence and fades. Just before the fence corner bear LEFT.

6 Now follow a rough stony track down beside the fence to a gate. Go down the field, later on an old track, to stone sheepfolds. Go down the next left-hand field edge to join a green track which descends to a stile/gate and crosses a stream. Keep ahead, soon being joined by another track. Follow it down to join your outward route to cross the stile by the gate.

7 Follow the track down beside the wooded valley, then down the wooded hillside to a minor road by a house.

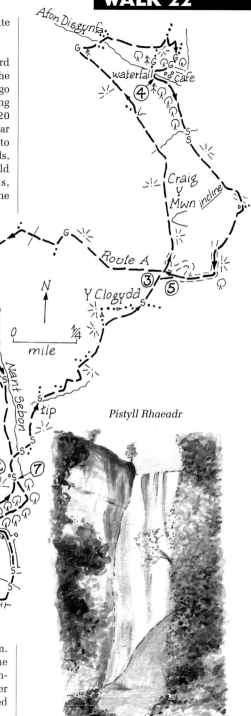

Pistyll Rhaeadr

Follow it LEFT, soon bending past a farm. On the next bend, cross a stile, follow the boundary round to another stile, then continue ahead to reach a quaint footbridge over the river. Turn RIGHT and follow the stiled riverside path to Llangynog.

WALK 23
LLANGYNOG

DESCRIPTION A varied 2¼ mile walk passing beneath Craig Rhiwarth, through woodland, with a delightful riverside return. Allow about 2 hours. See **Walk 22** map.
START Llangynog car park SJ 054262.

I Follow instructions in paragraph **1** of **Walk 22**, then at the stile/gate do a U-turn and follow text in paragraph **7**.

WALK 24
MOEL CRYNDDYN

DESCRIPTION A 4½ mile walk up the attractive Sebon side valley to the top of Moel Crynddyn (1656 feet), and a riverside return Allow about 3 hours. See **Walk 22** map.
START Llangynog car park SJ 054262.

I Follow instructions in paragraph **1** of **Walk 22**.

2 Cross the stile into Open Access land and follow the green track up the valley, later taking its left fork to go through a gate by sheepfolds. Bear RIGHT through a fence gap, then LEFT up the slope to follow a fence on your right through bracken. Continue up open ground, then bear LEFT up a track. At the top, near old workings, continue RIGHT up the track. At its end head up to the nearby summit of Moel Crynddyn, then return down to follow the nearby fence north to its corner. Cross the facing fence and bear RIGHT, then follow instructions in paragraphs **6** and **7** of **Walk 22**.

WALK 25
THE BERWYN ROUND

DESCRIPTION A challenging 13 mile walk for experienced walkers to the highest peaks of the Berwyn range, offering extensive views. The walk ascends to Cadair Berwyn (2722 feet) as in **Walk 26**, then continues along the ridge to Moel Sych (2712 feet), before making a delightful long steady descent along a wide moorland ridge to Milltir Gerrig. After descending a track into Cwm Ceidiog, it follows a quiet road back to Llandrillo. Allow about 8 hours. Avoid in poor visibility. A small former quarry (SJ 017306) just off the B4391 near the Powys road sign about 3½ miles north west of Llangynog, offers an alternative start, or a high start (1607 feet) for a straightforward 8 miles long steady ascent to Cadair Berwyn and back.
START Llandrillo SJ 035372. See **Walk 26**.

I - 3 Follow instructions in paragraphs **1-3** of **Walk 26** to the trig point then nearby craggy top on Cadair Berwyn.

4 Descend south to a ladder-stile and go along the ridge towards Moel Sych. After a peaty flattish section, take a path angling away from the edge to follow the nearby fence up to cross a ladder-stile on the wide flat top of Moel Sych to the small cairn just beyond. Continue on a permissive path signposted to Milltir Gerrig, with the fence to your right, down the wide moorland ridge. After about 1½ miles, the path passes a cairn and continues south west on a steady descent. After a short steeper descent, the path continues across the heather moorland towards the B4391 to eventually reach a stone track by a Y Berwyn Nature Reserve information board. (The path opposite leads to the quarry.)

5 Follow the track RIGHT down to a forest. Continue with the track down to cross a footbridge over a river, and on past nearby houses. Now simply follow the attractive narrow road along Cwm Ceidiog to Llandrillo.

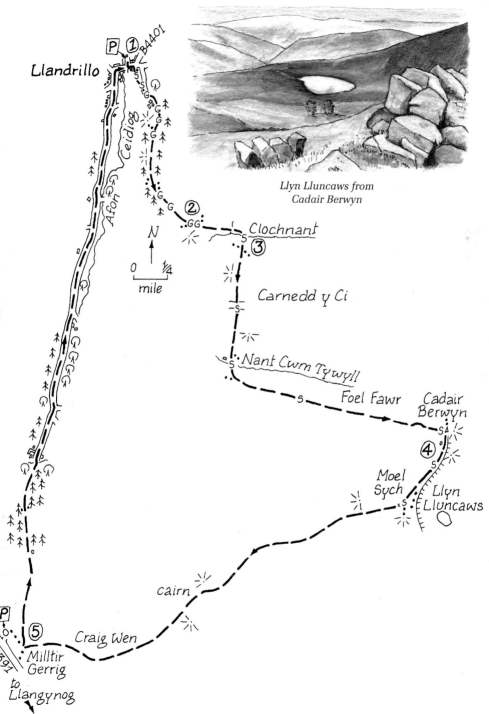

Llandrillo

B4401

N

0   ¼
mile

Afon Ceidiog

Llyn Lluncaws from
Cadair Berwyn

② GG

Clochnant

③

Carnedd y Ci

Nant Cwm Tywyll

Foel Fawr

Cadair
Berwyn

④

Moel
Sych

Llyn
Lluncaws

cairn

⑤ Craig Wen

Milltir
Gerrig

to
Llangynog

A4391

31

WALK 26

CADAIR BERWYN & CADAIR BRONWEN

DESCRIPTION A challenging 10 mile mountain walk (**A**) from Llandrillo for experienced walkers. The route climbs in stages to the top of Cadair Berwyn (2722 feet), continues north along the ridge then descends to Bwlch Maen Gwynedd. After a short climb to Cadair Bronwen (2558 feet), with an alternative bridleway **route B**, it returns via an impressive stone circle and an old drovers' route. Allow about 6 hours. Avoid in poor visibility. An alternative 7¾ mile walk (**B**) via Cwm Clochnant, wet in places, direct to Bwlch Maen Gwynedd and Cadair Bronwen is included.

START Llandrillo SH 035372.

DIRECTIONS Llandrillo lies on the on the former Corwen-Bala turnpike road, now the B4401. The riverside car park is in the village centre, near the 18thC stone bridge.

1 Return to the road and turn LEFT. Take a signposted path on the right past the side of Y Ganolfwyn and behind bungalows, then go half-LEFT across a field to a stile/gate in the corner onto a lane. Follow it RIGHT. After a gate continue up the stony track to Llechwedd. Keep ahead up a green track to a gate beneath the forest. The track now rises steadily along the forest edge, passing through two further gates. Later continue up the forestry track's left fork. When the track does a U-turn just beyond the forest end, go through the lower of two gates ahead. Follow the green track up to a gate into open country and on to go through another gate where you join a stony track.

2 Go to another gate ahead to enter Y Berwyn National Nature Reserve. Follow the green track ahead. After crossing a stream continue with a path parallel with the Clochnant. Shortly descend to cross the river and the ladder-stile above. (For **Walk B** con-tinue on an intermittent path above the river, later crossing a side stream. Just before a fence the path bends up to go through a gate. The path continues past a small forest and follows the Clochnant up the valley, later climbing to reach Bwlch Maen Gwynedd. Turn LEFT and resume instructions in paragraph **5**.)

3 Follow a path ahead across reedy ground. Ignore the green track angling up the slope, but continue on a path rising parallel with the nearby fence, soon through bracken. Later, the path continues across level ground to a ladder-stile, then contours across the lower slopes of Carnedd y Ci. As the path begins to bend up Cwm Tywyll, keep ahead to cross Nant Cwm Tywyll and a ladder-stile. Just beyond reeds follow a clear path up the slope to a waymark post. Turn LEFT and follow the path up the hillside. Later it levels out, crosses a ladder-stile, then continues across the broad ridge of Foel Fawr, before steadily climbing. The path disappears on the final ascent to a ladder-stile giving access to the trig point on Cadair Berwyn overlooking Cwm Maen Gwynedd. Follow the ridge path south down past a small pool, then up past a stone shelter to the small craggy top – *providing dramatic views down to Llyn Lluncaws, and extensive all-round views from the Welsh mountains to Cheshire and Shropshire.*

4 Return to the trig point and continue north along the ridge path. Later take the left fork to cross a ladder-stile. Follow the sleeper path west, then descend with the fence to a crossroad of paths at Bwlch Maen Gwynedd. (For **Route B**, turn LEFT down the path. After about 100 yards, take the right fork, soon contouring around the mid-slopes, then bending to cross the head of a side valley, and rising to join Route A at the fence.)

5 For **Route A** continue ahead up the path to cross a ladder-stile to reach the summit cairn on Cadair Berwyn. Re-cross the ladder-stile, then turn RIGHT and follow the fence down to join Route B. Follow the wide bridleway down near the fence. After a gate beneath Moel Pearce it heads north west down to another gate, then crosses rough

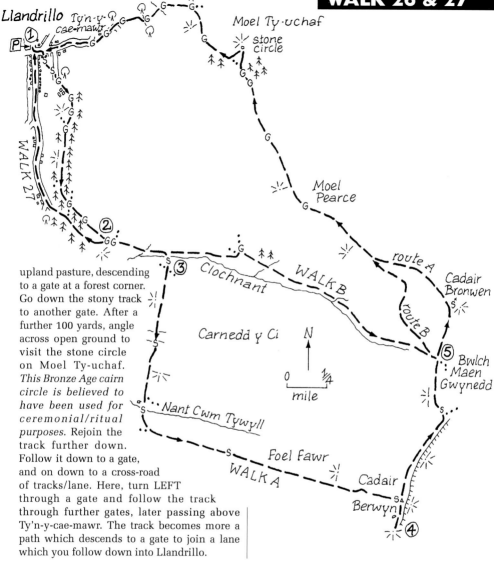

upland pasture, descending to a gate at a forest corner. Go down the stony track to another gate. After a further 100 yards, angle across open ground to visit the stone circle on Moel Ty-uchaf. *This Bronze Age cairn circle is believed to have been used for ceremonial/ritual purposes.* Rejoin the track further down. Follow it down to a gate, and on down to a cross-road of tracks/lane. Here, turn LEFT through a gate and follow the track through further gates, later passing above Ty'n-y-cae-mawr. The track becomes more a path which descends to a gate to join a lane which you follow down into Llandrillo.

WALK 27
BERWYN FRINGES

DESCRIPTION This 2¾ mile walk rises steadily past forest into open upland country (1236 feet) at the edge of the Berwyns, then descends to return along the attractive Ceidiog valley. Allow about 2 hours.
START Llandrillo SH 035372.

1 Follow instructions in paragraph **1** of Walk 26.

2 Here do a sharp U-turn and follow the stony track down through the forest, to join a minor road, which takes you along the Ceidiog valley back to Llandrillo.

WALK 28

CADAIR BRONWEN

DESCRIPTION A 10 mile walk for experienced walkers featuring two ancient upland passes and Cadair Berwyn (2558 feet), the most northern of the three peaks of the Berwyns. The route follows a good track, an ancient highway connecting the Dee and Ceiriog valleys, on a long steady climb to Pen Bwlch Llandrillo. A path now climbs in stages across moorland to Cadair Bronwen, with its panoramic all-round views, then descends to Bwlch Maen Gwynedd, returning via Cwm Clochnant, wet in places. Allow about 5 hours. Avoid in poor visibility.
START Llandrillo SH 035372
DIRECTIONS Llandrillo lies on the B4401. The riverside car park is signposted in the village centre.

1 Return to the main road and follow it LEFT. Just past the cenotaph, take the minor road on the right. It later rises to end at the entrance track to Ty'n Caer Mawr. Keep ahead up a stony track to go through a gate. Follow the old track up through trees. After passing above Ty'n Caer Mawr, continue ahead up the stony access track and through a gate. When the stony track bends right, keep ahead up a green track and through a gate – *with good views looking back along the Dee valley to Arenig.* Continue with the delightful track through two further gates. The track now climbs steadily to another gate at a cross-road of tracks/lane.

2 Keep ahead. The gated track rises past a small wood and continues into open country, later turning towards the Berwyn ridge. After passing a forest, the track descends to cross a stream. Keep with the main track, later steadily descending into the valley to reach an old stone bridge over the river – Pont Rhyd-yr-hydd. *A path on the right leads to a nearby waterfall and commemorative slate seat – a great place to stop.* Cross the bridge and continue up the stony track, past a strip of forest, and on up the hillside.

3 At a metal pole, a track joins from the left. Keep ahead to go through a gate by a ruin and follow the track up to Pen Bwlch Llandrillo. *To the left is a plaque dedicated to Wayfarer 1877-1956 – a lover of Wales erected by the RSF, with a metal box in front containing notebooks for recording comments.* Here take a path on the right waymarked to Cadair Bronwen. Follow the path south along the undulating moorland – *enjoying extensive views from the Ceiriog valley to Snowdonia* – later following a fence on a long steady climb up the hillside. The path levels out, crosses a ladder-stile, then makes a final ascent to the summit cairn on Cadair Bronwen – *offering extensive all-round views: from Cader Idris to Merseyside, from Snowdon to Shropshire. Cadair Berwyn lies ahead.* Cross the ladder-stile below, and follow the path down and across to a small gate at a crossroad of paths at Bwlch Maen Gwynedd.

4 Here turn RIGHT and follow the path down the slope. After about 100 yards, take the left fork. The path steadily descends into Cwm Clochnant, briefly joining the right bank of a small valley. After a deep rutted section of path, go half-RIGHT to follow a rutted track across reedy ground to join another path beneath the nearby heather covered slope. The path steadily descends, later running above the Clochnant, crosses two side streams and passes a small forest. After a gate, follow a path LEFT, soon bending RIGHT. Keep with the left fork. The path later fades as it crosses a wettish reedy area, then improves and suddenly descends to cross a side stream. The intermittent path continues following the nearby Clochnant. After passing a ladder-stile up on the opposite bank, you join a gradually improving path. After a stream, continue along a stony track to leave the Berwyn Nature Reserve at a gate/stile.

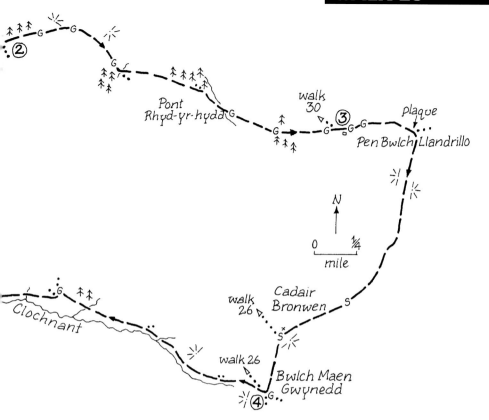

5 Leave the stony track at another gate ahead and follow a green track through two further gates, then continue down a forestry track. After a gate, keep with the right fork descending beneath the forest through two further gates, then follow the green track down to Llechwedd. Descend its access track, then follow the lane to a junction. Turn LEFT into Llandrillo.

About the author, David Berry

David is an experienced walker with a love of the countryside and an interest in local history. He is the author of a series of walks guidebooks covering North Wales, where he has lived and worked for many years, as well as a freelance writer for Walking Wales magazine. He has worked as a Rights of Way surveyor across North Wales and served as a member of Denbighshire Local Access Forum.

Whether on a riverside ramble, mountain or long distance walk, he greatly appreciates the beauty, culture and history of the landscape and hopes that his comprehensive guidebooks will encourage people to explore on foot its diverse scenery and rich heritage.

Pont Rhyd-yr-hydd

WALK 29
MOEL TY UCHAF CIRCLE

DESCRIPTION A 4½ mile walk following an ancient track up to a Bronze Age ceremonial stone circle on Moel Ty Uchaf (1443 feet), returning via 18thC Hendwr. Allow about 3 hours.
START Llandrillo SJ 035371. **See Walk 28.**

1 Follow instructions in paragraph **1** of **Walk 28** to a crossroad of tracks/lane. Turn RIGHT and follow the track up the hillside, through a gate, later leaving it to visit the stone circle on Moel Ty Uchaf. Return down the track then follow the lane down to the B4401. Follow it RIGHT over the river, then go along a lane on the left, past a house.

2 Just beyond an old barn, turn LEFT along an enclosed track. Later on a bend, cross a stile to enter Hendwr caravan park. Continue along its edge then cross a footbridge over the river. Just past the toilet/utility block, turn RIGHT, then LEFT to follow a track past caravans. Cross an access lane and go through a gate ahead. Go past a large barn, then angle LEFT to go through a gate by another barn. *The nearby imposing 18thC house reflects the importance of the Hendwr estate, standing at the junction of ancient valley and mountain routes. For many centuries it has been associated with prominent Welsh families.* Continue ahead past a modern house to go through a waymarked gate beyond trees. Now follow a waymarked stiled path through several fields, then go along a short hedge-lined green track to a stile near a house. Angle LEFT across the large field to cross a stile by sewerage works, and another just beyond. Follow the lane to the start.

Moel Ty Uchaf

WALK 30
PONT RHYD-YR-HYDD

DESCRIPTION An exhilarating 9½ mile walk exploring the Upper Dee Valley between Cynwyd and Llandrillo. The route follows scenic ancient upland trackways around the foothills of the Berwyns, reaching a height of 1600 feet and offering panoramic views. These former important highways across the Berwyns connected the Dee and Ceiriog valleys. The route returns through attractive undulating countryside and past 18thC Hendwr. Allow about 5½ hours.
START Llandrillo SJ 035371.

1 Follow instructions in paragraphs **1** and **2** of **Walk 28**.

2 At a metal post swing sharp LEFT along another stony track and through a gate. The track now contours across the open slopes, before steadily descending to pass through a gate by Scots pines. Keep on with the track to join a tarmaced road by a large barn. Just beyond, take a green track angling away on the right. Follow the gated track across the slope then down the hillside, past a barn and down to a lane at the entrance to Henfaes Isaf. Continue down the lane. After a gate cross a barred stile on the left opposite a forked access track.

3 Descend to cross the stream. Go half-LEFT up the field to cross another barred stile. Keep ahead past gorse and variable bracken to reach a waymark post by a large tree. Continue across the grassland plateau before gently descending to another waymark post on the left. Follow the path through bracken to a kissing gate. Ignore the adjoining stile, but continue ahead alongside the forest. Later follow a green track to a road.

4 Go down the green track opposite on a steady descent to a farm. Continue along its access lane, then follow the minor road for ½ mile to the B4401. Follow the road LEFT and after ¼ mile, turn RIGHT along a lane, past a house. Now follow instructions in paragraph **2** of **Walk 29** back to Llandrillo.

1 From the Post Office/store go along the main road past the Prince of Wales, then take the minor road on the left. Follow it to cross the river, then immediately turn LEFT to follow a narrow road rising steadily above the wooded side valley. About 50 yards after passing a farm, take a signposted path over a stile on the right. The short tree-lined path leads to another stile, then continues across a field passing close to a wood on your left.

2 Just before its corner, the path moves away from the fence to cross a stream to go through a small gate above. Continue across the next field to cross a stile in the right-hand corner. Turn right along the lane past Pant y Gai cottage to take the left fork to reach another narrow lane. Cross the barred stile opposite.

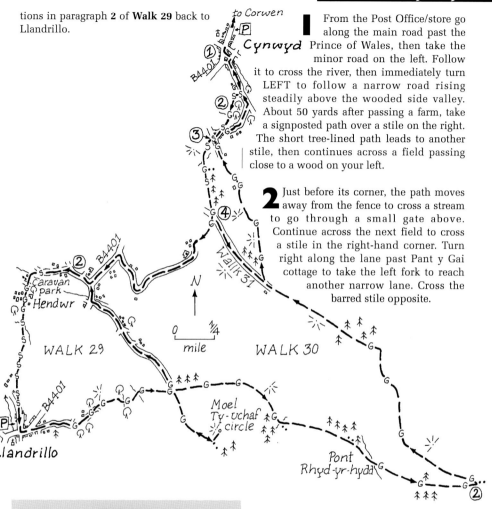

WALK 31
SOUTH OF CYNWYD

DESCRIPTION A 3¾ mile walk exploring the undulating countryside near Cynwyd. The route rises in stages via quiet lanes and field paths to the edge of open country at 1180 feet, before returning on a delightful ancient upland trackway – offering extensive views – and lanes. Allow about 2½ hours.
START Cynwyd SJ 057411.
DIRECTIONS Cynwyd lies on the B4401.

3 Follow instructions in section **3** of **Walk 30**.

4 Go up the road – *later enjoying good views to the Arans, Arenig and the Carneddau*. After passing a forest, where the road levels out just before a barn, take a green track angling back on the left. Follow the gated track across the slope then down the hillside, past a barn and down to a lane at the entrance to Henfaes Isaf. Follow the lane down. After a gate you rejoin your outward route. After passing Pant y Gai cottage now continue with the gated lane past houses to a junction. Turn LEFT back to Cynwyd.

WALK 32

CORWEN – LLIDIART Y PARC

CORWEN

River Dee

Llangar Church

N

0 ¼ mile

Cynwyd

DESCRIPTION A 10 mile linear walk for experienced walkers featuring the first section of the North Berwyn Way (NBW) to Moel Fferna (2066 feet), offering panoramic views. After a better alternative start than the A5, the route follows the NBW past medieval Llangar church to Cynwyd. After climbing steadily up a wooded valley, the NBW passes through sections of forest then crosses expansive heather moorland to the summit of Moel Fferna. After descending its northern slopes, the route follows a waymarked NBW link path down the moorland and through a forest to Llidiart-y-Parc, from where paths take you to the A5 near the start. Allow about 5 hours.

START Corwen SJ 079435.

DIRECTIONS First park in a long lay-by on the A5 ¼ mile west of Llidiart-y-Parc (SJ 118433). Walk east along the pavement to the bus stop on the south side of the road. Take the regular X94 Chester-Barmouth bus or more limited X19 bus to Corwen. (Traveline Cymru 0871 200 22 33)

*C*orwen *was once an important crossing point for traders and drovers, then a key stopping place on the stagecoach route, now the A5, to and from Ireland via Holyhead. After the arrival of the railway in the mid 19thC it developed as a flourishing market town. The area is associated with Owain Glyndŵr, one of the heroes of Welsh history, who led a sustained campaign against English rule at the beginning of the 15thC. He had a house at Llidiart-y-Parc.*

From Owain Glyndŵr's statue in Corwen town centre, head west along the High Street. Cross the road at the Pelican crossing, then go up Penybryn past the side of HSBC bank. When it bends left go half-RIGHT down a lane past Brynawelon. At its end follow a narrow path down to the A5, then above the road up through trees. Immediately beyond a waymark post, turn RIGHT down a stepped path through the trees to the A5/B4401 junction. Turn LEFT, then take the signposted path (NBW) by the road sign opposite, soon joining a stony track. Shortly, cross a stile to the right of the gated entrance to Troed-y-Bryn, and continue along the riverside edge of landscaped gardens. At their end, cross a stile and walk along a wooded section of the former Corwen-Bala railway line, now a nature reserve.

2 At a signposted path junction by a house, for a visit to nearby 13thC Llangar Church, go through the kissing gate, along a track, then through a gate on the left to the church. Return to the path junction. Continue with the NBW along the former railway embankment. After about ½ mile cross a stile on the left and go along the edge of three fields to a stile and up the tree-lined path to the B4401. Follow it RIGHT into Cynwyd.

38

3 From the village centre take the minor road past the side of The Blue Lion. At a junction, keep ahead on the No through road. The narrow road climbs steadily past houses and along the wooded valley, then continues up through the forest to eventually level out at a cottage. Just beyond go up a track on the left. At the junction, turn RIGHT, then take the left fork up through the forest. Continue with the green track along the forest edge to its end at a stile. Now follow a path across open ground, then through another section of forest to eventually join a track. Follow it LEFT, past a track on the left (Liberty Hall) and up through the forest to cross a stile at its edge. Keep ahead to follow a green track across the expansive moorland – *with views south to the Berwyns, and ahead to Moel Fferna* – later rising in stages to eventually reach a gate in a fence. Here, turn LEFT follow the NBW path up to a stile on the ridge. (The NBW continues east along the ridge.)

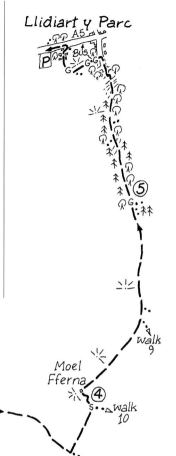

4 Bear LEFT along the track and on through a peaty area to reach two stone shelters on the top of Moel Fferna. Take a path heading NE, then follow either the stony path or a rough track down the heather hillside – *with a view across to two former slate quarries (see Walk 9)* – to reach a waymark post at a path junction. Here bear LEFT and follow a delightful green track (a link section of the NBW) on a long steady descent across moorland to eventually reach a gate at the corner of a forest.

5 Follow the green track along the edge of the forest, soon descending in stages to a forestry track. After a few yards, take the waymarked path angling down on the left. The green track descends through mixed woodland, later becoming more of a path, to eventually join another forestry track. The waymarked path descends to another track below, then descends through trees and continues down a track past The Dell. Just before another house, take a signposted path on the left to cross a stream. After a gate follow the green track to another gate. The track rises with good views across the Dee valley to Carrog to join another track. Follow it down to pass through a farm to reach the A5. Cross the road with care and follow the pavement back to the lay-by.

PRONUNCIATION

Welsh	English equivalent
c	always hard, as in cat
ch	as in the Scottish word loch
dd	as th in then
f	as f in of
ff	as ff in off
g	always hard as in got
ll	no real equivalent. It is like 'th' in then, but with an 'L' sound added to it, giving 'thlan' for the pronunciation of the Welsh 'Llan'.

In Welsh the accent usually falls on the last-but-one syllable of a word.

KEY TO THE MAPS

- ➤ Walk route and direction
- Metalled road
- Unsurfaced road
- +++ Fence
- •••• Footpath/route adjoining walk route
- River/stream
- Trees
- Rocks
- G Gate
- S Stile
- F.B. Footbridge
- Viewpoint
- M Summit

Useful information

Wrexham Bus Line: 01978 266166 or **Traveline Cymru** 0871 200 22 33 for details of the regular bus service operating along the Ceiriog Valley, giving access to the walks.
Wrexham County Borough Rights of Way: 01978 292057 – re: any problems in the Ceiriog Valley.
Chirk Castle: (01691 777701 or www.nationaltrust.org.uk)

THE COUNTRYSIDE CODE

- Be safe – plan ahead and follow any signs
- Leave gates and property as you find them
- Protect plants and animals, and take your litter home
- Keep dogs under close control
- Consider other people

Open Access

Some routes cross areas of land where walkers have the legal right of access under The CRoW Act 2000 introduced in May 2005. Access can be subject to restrictions and closure for land management or safety reasons for up to 28 days a year. Details from: www.naturalresourceswales.gov.uk.
Please respect any notices.

Published by **Kittiwake Books Limited**
3 Glantwymyn Village Workshops, Glantwymyn, Machynlleth, Montgomeryshire SY20 8LY

© Text & map research: David Berry 2008
www.davidberrywalks.co.uk

© Maps & illustrations: Kittiwake 2008
Drawings by Morag Perrott
Cover photos: Main – The Berwyn from Craig y Mwn (Walk 22) – David Berry. *Inset* – The West Arms.

Care has been taken to be accurate. However neither the author nor the publisher can accept responsibility for any errors which may appear, or their consequences. If you are in any doubt about access, check before you proceed.

Printed by Mixam, UK.

ISBN: **978 1 902302 62 1**